These Small Hours

Rachel Donaldson

BookLeaf Publishing

These Small Hours © 2022 Rachel Donaldson

All rights reserved.

No part of this publication may be reproduced, stored in a retrieval system, or transmitted, in any form or by any means, electronic, mechanical, photocopying, recording or otherwise, without the prior written permission of the presenters.

Rachel Donaldson asserts the moral right to be identified as author of this work.

Presentation by *BookLeaf Publishing*

Web: www.bookleafpub.com

E-mail: info@bookleafpub.com

ISBN: 9789395969154

First edition 2022

To my parents, I love you more.

To my kids, Ranin and Zai-Anne, you're my world. Always believe in yourself.

To my partner, thank you for everything. I love you forever and always.

ACKNOWLEDGEMENT

I'd like to acknowledge the amazing support I've received from Justin (my partner), Charity, Nysa, Laura & Tianna.

Thank you for always being there and supporting me in my endeavors. It means the world to me and I wouldn't be where I am without you guys. I love you.

PREFACE

Dear Reader,

I guess, I wrote this book on a whim if I'm being honest. I've never written a book, I don't have any credentials. I simply wanted to challenge myself to do something new and maybe, just maybe get some of these feelings out.

In this book, I want to share a wide range of poetry from various points in my life. I've faced my fair share of challenges (addiction and abuse among other things). This isn't a recovery story, or a "things always get better" type of book. I just want to share some of my words with you and I hope you enjoy them.

That's it. That's all.

If you do take the time to read this, then thank you so much. I appreciate it. I wish you all nothing but the best.

Love,

Rachel Ebony

I'll Try To Explain

They all come in clips.
Never more than a second long.
But always bright.

Fractals passing by.
Glimpses into the far past.
Often left breathless.

Then my brain turns to static.
Why can't I focus?

Flashing vividly.
Forever changing channels.
I wish I could pause.

Could I remember?
More than fractals and smoke?
Close my eyes and try.

How I Met Her

I saw her on the bus.
He hair a soft ebony.
No make up. Brown eyes.
I could drown in them.
Her laugh fills my head, echoing for what seems
like eternity.
She smiles. It's warm. It's inviting.
She said something.

Tan and pretty.
Took my breath away.
Tan and pretty.
Stands out in this crowded and cramped space.

Her lips move. She seems to glow.
I'm snapped back to reality. I'll never forget
those words.

"HEY! THAT NEW KID HAS A NAME!"

You Came Back

3

Happy fractals.
Standing on a hill; warm and bright.
Your green jacket. Old and worn, heading my
way.
My heart could burst. My chest is so tight with
joy.
I want to hold this moment.
"It's a happy cry."
I want to hold this feeling and never let go.

If only I could pick these moments like flowers.

I Blinked

So much smoke,
such a tiny sphere.
An entirely different perspective.
Only held in for a moment,
yet can steal a lifetime.
The feeling of a rush.
Incapable of sleep.
A slight madness lingers,
a thought forever changed.
The evidence leaking through the skin.
The thirst for pure substance.
Any and all hunger is non-existent.
The beating of the love organ quickens.
Suddenly there are so many more things to look
at.
More alert. More aware.
All in those few seconds.
Just one inhale followed by the exhale.
Just that tiny sphere,
filled with all that smoke,
forever changes the appearance of the universe.

Lost in Time

The smoke that flooded the room clears.

The thoughts just begin to flood the crammed space.

Not quite claustrophobic, not too crowded to stay.

One thought blends into another.

A different kind of smoke lingering in this room.

Not too dark to see through; a transparency remains, though not as much as to allow a clear view.

Yet, this smoke is somewhat invited.

It swirls in circles overhead, not stopping to allow intricate details to be seen.

Not wanting a total focus on itself.

The steady beat faint in your ears; a bit faster than normal.

Seems to keep up with the slow tornado, this smoke swirling so gracefully.

It brings a grin to the surface. The kind of grin a child has on a merry go ground.

The rush feels like an amusement ride.

Slowly the smoke dwindles away. No more unfocusable tornadoes.

Suck back slow.

Flood the room with more smoke to watch it fade and then flood the room some more.

The thoughts.

The lingering smoke.

The beginning of the ride.

4:30 a.m.

7

Shifting gears; four thirty a.m.
Spaced moments; mostly enjoyable.
Not tired at all; just not all there.

12:00 a.m.

There are some tiny moments drenched in fear.
Let's call them midnight hours.
God, they seemed like hours.
Hours.
Frozen in time.
My insides seem to shrivel inwards the first
time.
But they never seem to come back.
Disconnected my circuits the second time.
Cold. Numb.
Strange.
Am I breathing?
Why can't I move?
Numb.
I twitch. You vacate.
It's over till the next time.
So entitled.

We don't belong to you.

Silence

I wish silence didn't hurt.
I wish silence was quiet.
I wish I could hear over the static.
I wish it didn't make me anxious; panic.
I wish it didn't make me afraid.
I wish it didn't pull me down.
I wish I didn't need to talk to myself to fill the void.
I wish it would bring calmness.
I wish chaos didn't feel so good.
I wish my body didn't ache from being so tense.
I wish I could turn it off.
I wish I could hear you the first time.

I wish I could hear over the static.

Shadows

Twisting and forming in the light of flame.
Touching and fleeing like some childhood game.
Licking the blank canvas made of wall.
The shadows seem eager to taste it all.
To be a shadow seems so carefree.
At least, on the surface that's what I see.
The life of a shadow is all to short yet sweet.
For they die when with darkness they meet.
Or is that truly so?
Is there so much more the surface doesn't show?

Machines

Image after image.
Sound after sound.
Feeling after feeling.
Beat after beat.
Never ending thoughts, one dissolving into
another.
Not a blank moment. Even the blankness is a
thought in itself, so hard to hold.
The thought fades into another.
The wheels are always turning.
So consistently, it's almost robotic.
Carried by wires and fed to the brain.
Connecting the dots.
Programming the image, the sound, feeling and
beat.
Humans. Fleshy mechanical puppets.
Always trying to perform as told.

The answer we seek is not the mechanics or
function.

Do you hold control? Are you a puppet to your
soul?

Question?

Art; is it all paintings and drawings?
Or could the ink on this page, even if only
forming such familiar markings as "letters" and
"words," be considered art as well?

After all, it's ink and paper as many masterpieces
are.
If a single dot on paper is "insightful" or "deep,"
and considered art by some, then couldn't the
mere lines and dots on this page be art too?
Could this be "deep" and "insightful," as well?

Why are these ink formations called letters,
words, and used to communicate?
It is after all mere ink on paper.
Why does a drawing not form specific sounds
for every line or colour present?

Art speaks on other volumes, and differently to
many people.
But why is it not considered words as well?
Could it all be art that has it's own voice?
Speaking out differently, communicating
differently.

Neither one heard through ears, but heard by
eyes.

13

5:00 a.m.

Irratic thoughts flood the brain.
An overflow of subconscious riddles.
Solving them seems much too impossible.
An attempt to solve one's self,
Leaving a mess of confusion in its path.
Mixed feelings surface.
Helplessness takes over.
The downward spiral begins.

I don't want to stop it.

Clouds

15

One after the other.

Fading faster than the sunlight in winter.

Each breath sending us higher into oblivion.

Thoughts race a million miles a second.

Eyes shift directions faster than the thoughts.

Words spill out, words that come out faster than
the thoughts.

Sketching. Tripping. All together building up
insanity.

Emotions, opinions and nonsense flooding into
the open air.

More clouds. More thoughts into words.

Speeding like a rocketship bound for the next
galaxy.

Mind blown open.

Always welcoming those clouds.

Those unmistakable clouds.

The ones that fade faster than the sunlight in winter.

The same ones that come and fade one after the other.

Late Night.. Or Early Morning.

Time so slow, almost at a stand still.
Eerie creaks, faintly heard.
Completely aware but not all there.
Silence, a decadent design.
Night atmosphere, the numbing backdrop.
A faint purr, a comfort.
A light breathing sound, a sleeping love.
A brush of warmth, a reassurance.
Television on, a drown out nightlight.
Another thought come and gone.
And a few more, passing time.
Listen to a heartbeat, sense of reality.
Faint red numbers glowing, a therapeutic
moment.
A slight move, a change of contour.
A feeling of longing.
Another brush of warmth stolen quietly.

The only time I will remember you fondly.

I Want To Sleep

Dreams are my savior.
Save me now.
Save me forever.

Opaque

Blank faces, painted up to disguise.

Blank stares, somehow cutting into your skin.

One false personality made of lace.

So distorted, no recognition.

A seemingly lifeless body so horrifically
contorted.

The image so twisted with a background not so
much black as misted.

Sick, dark thoughts so beautifully
choreographed.

Out of this void a monster is born.

New to this world so cold and alone.

Nothing tastes better than a damaged brain.
"You're already dead girl, you won't feel the
pain."

This is the scene overflowing with gore.
"Sick, little child - I know you want more."
"Dear child, don't you know?"
You are this creature so disgustingly low.

Confusion.

Blank stares. Blank faces, staring back at me in
the mirror.

Paulette, Wherever You Are....

You're terribly missed.

The sun isn't as bright without you.
The flowers don't seem to bloom as brilliantly.
The leaves don't fall the same.
The snow is not as fluffy since you've gone.
The birds don't sound as sweet.
The stars though, have shone more vividly than
ever.

P.S. Wear the carousel earrings.

Sometime Late

22

I wonder what happens when stars and
chemicals collide.
I wonder if it's anything like being under these
lights with you.
I wonder if they feel the impact.
Do they entwine?
I wonder if they burn so bright it's blinding.
Will they fade?
Will they lose themselves?
Is there anything left in the aftermath?

I wonder what happens when stars and
chemicals collide.

In The Final Hours

23

I hope to find peace.
I hope to be loved.
I hope to have happiness.
I hope to be really alive.

I hope that for you too.